THE LEPRECHAUN
LIBRARY

HERITAGE OF FLOWERS

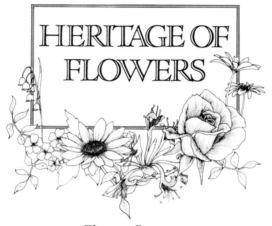

Eleanor Bourne
Illustrated by Alan Baker

HUTCHINSON
London Melbourne Sydney Auckland Johannesburg

POPPY

The poppy's various overlapping meanings come together in the Greek myth of Demeter and Persephone. Demeter was the goddess of the earth, the fruitfulness of which is strongly associated with the cornfields. Here the brilliant poppy has always flourished, and for this reason Demeter is commonly represented with poppies and corn in her hands.

Demeter's daughter Persephone was wandering one day in a meadow, picking flowers. Suddenly the earth opened up and Hades, god of the Underworld, emerged to carry her off to the Underworld to be his wife. Not knowing of her daughter's fate, Demeter wandered the earth searching for her. In rage and despair when she discovered what had happened to her, Demeter forbad the earth to bear fruit until her daughter was returned. Faced with this threat to mankind Zeus instructed Hades to return Persephone. There was one condition: that Persephone should not have eaten of the food of the dead of the Underworld. Persephone returned but it was revealed that she had eaten some pomegranite seeds. So it was agreed that Persephone would have to return to Hades for three months of each year and would be restored to earth for the remaining nine. So the earth suffers for three months of winter when the crops will not grow. Then, with the return of Persephone, spring comes.

Legends say that Persephone was picking poppies when she was abducted. The poppy has always had associations with sleep and therefore stands for the dormant earth when Persephone is absent. The colour of the flower, too, a flaming red, is another symbol – of resurrection from the dead. With Persephone's return each year the earth comes triumphantly back to life. Embodiment of sleep, resurrection and fruitfulness, the poppy was one of the most potent symbols of the ancient world.

THEY SHALL NOT
GROW OLD, AS WE
THAT ARE LEFT
GROW OLD;

AGE SHALL NOT WEARY
THEM, NOR THE
YEARS CONDEMN.

AT THE GOING DOWN
OF THE SUN AND IN
THE MORNING

WE WILL
REMEMBER THEM.

Recent developments in iris breeding that have been so successful in the creation of new plants with the most subtle of colour shadings make the name of the flower more appropriate than ever before. Iris, bearer of messages from Olympus to the earth, travelled so frequently between the two that the rainbow became the bridge that helped her on these journeys. Iris is used as the name for the rainbow itself and for the flower that, even from its earliest days, has appeared in a beautiful variety of colours.

The simple yellow water iris, the 'flag' or the 'sword' that grows in river shallows and on pond edges, has won lasting fame as the emblem of the great royal houses of France and as a national symbol. The sixth-century king of the Franks, Clovis, began the cult. His army was trapped by the Goths when the Rhine barred the way ahead. Far out in the water he observed the yellow iris growing. The iris grows rooted in soil, so it was clear to Clovis that the water must have been very shallow at that point. Knowing this, he and his army were able to ford the river and escape their pursuers.

Clovis adopted the flower as his own. It was, however, his descendant Louis VII who gave it the popular title by which it has so long been known – *fleur de lys*. 'Lys' or alternatively 'luce' are both versions of the name of Louis. Stylized representations of the three-petalled device have frequently appeared in heraldry and works of art ever since.

SUNFLOWER

There is nothing far-fetched about the sunflower's name – it is nature's clear, dramatic copy of the flaming sun itself. A flamboyant giant of the Americas, it was a sacred food plant of the prairie Indians. Its rich, oil-bearing seeds were only one of its attractions. Fibre and petals, too, could be put to use and North America's European immigrants soon learned of its virtues.

But it was further south in the Peru of the Incas where the sunflower, symbol of the great sun god, came into its own. Sun and sunflower alike, both in lavish supply, were represented in the pure gold that blessed this rich civilization. Great sunflowers made of gold were carried by the virgins who officiated at the rituals of the temples of the sun. For the sixteenth-century Spanish invaders of the New World, the sight of these dazzling artefacts was shattering.

The sunflower's more recent associations seem modest by comparison. Le Roi Soleil, Louis XIV, had a penchant for the flower for its obvious connections with his chosen role. More recently, in England, came the nineteenth-century Aesthetic Movement, led by Oscar Wilde, which adopted the sunflower as its symbol and incorporated it into buildings, fabrics and all the decorative art under its influence.

DIANTHUS

Carnations, gillyflowers, pinks – all charming members of the dianthus family – have been loved, bred and documented for centuries in England. Among pictorial tributes is a delightful miniature portrait of a five-year-old girl demurely holding a single red carnation, painted by Isaac Oliver in 1590. Then there are dozens of evocative names, ranging from 'Master Tuggie's princess' to 'pheasant's eye' and from 'painted lady' to 'Mrs Sinkins'. Even the early florists' show classes are beautifully named: flakes, bizarres and picotees. The pursuit of perfection gave rise to men being hired just to 'dress and lay out' carnations for exhibition.

A great wave of interest hit the pink world in the 1830s and 1840s. In Paisley, Scotland, weavers of the famous shawls flocked to the Florists' Club and devoted their free time to the development of the laced pink. Their single-minded enthusiasm produced eighty different varieties that were shown and judged in the 'Annual and Amicable Competition' of the club. The nonconformist severity of the time and place is supposed to account for this passion for pinks. Whatever the motivation, the outcome is sad. Not one of the famous 'laced pinks of Paisley' has survived. They are just part of botanical history.

The dianthus features in romantic history, too. Marie Antoinette, victim of the French Revolution, was visited in prison by the Chevalier de Rougeville, who had plans to rescue her. Written on a scrap of paper, they were concealed inside a carnation that he casually dropped. But her gaolers were not totally inept. The plot failed and she went to her death.

ROSE

The rose, a universal flower, has long been celebrated in art and poetry, and grown throughout the world on royal estates, in simple gardens and in wild hedgerows. It stands for medieval romance and modern lovers; for war and peace; for the pagan and the Christian; for Greece and Rome; for York and Lancaster, and finally for England. One early French romance describes how knights-in-armour stormed a castle occupied by fair damsels whose only weapons were the roses they showered down on the invaders.

The warring factions of York and Lancaster picked the white rose and the red as their emblems before embarking on the struggle known to every schoolboy as the Wars of the Roses. Although the Lancastrians were the victors, the marriage of their Henry to Elizabeth of York brought unity and peace, symbolized in the device created for the new royal house: the Tudor rose flaunting both red and white petals – united for England.

The rose has also been unofficially adopted by several American states, among them Georgia, Texas, New York, Iowa, North Dakota and the District of Columbia.

In France the rose has decorative rather than political associations. Both Madame de Pompadour and Madame du Barry, mistresses of Louis XV, revelled in roses. In celebrated portraits, each appears surrounded by a profusion of the lovely blooms. But it was Empress Joséphine, Napoleon's wife, whose devotion to roses was most tangibly displayed. As well as growing them in the famous garden she created at Malmaison, she commissioned Redouté, the 'Raphael of the Rose', to paint his renowned rose portraits. Sadly, his great book, *Les Roses*, was not published until after Joséphine's death; and it was dedicated not to her but to the restored Bourbon, the Duchesse d'Orléans.

CHRISTMAS ROSE

All the hellebores have tales to tell, not least because of their medicinal strength. One Gilbert White of Selborne commented as follows on the plants' ability to cure children's worms: 'Where it killed not the patient, it would certainly kill the worms; but the worst of it is, it will sometimes kill both.' Hellebores were also used as a purge, a cattle cure and a treatment for insanity. But the story of *Helleborus niger* – the famous Christmas rose – has more pleasant associations. According to an old mystery play, Madelon, a simple peasant girl, came to the stable in Bethlehem with the Shepherds but had no present for the baby Jesus. She thought of flowers, but none were blooming in the deep mid-winter. An angel took pity on her and touched the snowy ground, creating a beautiful flower. It was the Christmas rose, beloved ever since in its rôle as the first flower to brave the winter.

TULIP

One of the fundamental reasons why the tulip has had such a frenzied commercial history is because of its habit of 'breaking': a basic tulip, called a breeder, will suddenly change and produce a different flower in which the colours are either 'feathered' (streaked) or 'flamed'. This process is quite unpredictable and it has only recently been discovered that the cause is a virus infection. These beautiful chance colour changes help to explain why the phenomenon of 'tulipomania' swept Holland in the seventeenth century.

The tulip was originally cultivated in Turkey and its name is based on its similarity to the Turkish *dulband* or turban. When bulbs from this source began to trickle into the Netherlands, the florists and plantsmen got to work and before long the mania took over.

Between 1634 and 1637 a passion gripped the Dutch. Bulbs changed hands for extravagant sums, for carriages and pairs, for acres of land. The famous *Semper Augustus*, a bulb that flowered scarlet and white, flamed rose, changed hands for 5,500 florins. Nor was it just the bulbs: speculators moved in and sold promissory notes – paper tulips that did not yet exist but depended on a future 'break'. Horror stories abound too. An ignorant seaman ate a precious imported bulb with his herring supper. Some bulbs were brought only to be destroyed, in order to protect the exclusivity of another. Eventually, of course, the frenzy abated. But the tulip has become part of the nation's heritage, celebrated in the beautiful Dutch flower paintings of the seventeenth century and in the country's world-famous bulb-growing industry, which has flourished for over three hundred years.

DAFFODIL

Narcissus – family name for all the daffodils, jonquils and narcissi of our spring gardens – is called after the beautiful boy of that name. Proud of his looks and his success in love, he rejected the advances of the nymph Echo. The gods looked on him with disfavour and arranged that he fall passionately in love with his own reflection in clear spring water. Thus he was denied all hope of consummation. He languished there by the water till his death, when he was transformed into the sweet spring flower that bears his name.

'Narcissus' and 'narcotic' have the same etymological origin and there is a tradition that the smell of the first has the effect of the second. But, throughout those many centuries when plants were grown primarily for their culinary or medicinal properties, no use was found for narcissi or daffodils.

It is interesting to find that the gardens of the early Puritan settlers in seventeenth-century New England had no place for these purely ornamental bulbous plants. Life was hard and a garden plant had to earn its keep.

So, though far from exotic or over-refined, either in wild or cultivated forms, the daffodils have always been welcomed and admired for their looks alone. Celebrated by a host of English poets, one of the best-known descriptions comes from a nursery rhyme: "Daffy-down-dilly has come up to town, in her yellow petticoat and her green gown."

DELPHINIUM

Delphinium is the family name of both wild larkspur, which had already been brought into English gardens and cultivated by the time of Elizabeth I, and its showy twentieth-century cousin, the hybridized flower which forms the dressy bright blue backdrop to so many herbaceous borders.

However, the larkspur's botanical name *Delphinium ajacis* is the key to its romantic origins, set in the period of the Trojan War. Ajax, son of Telamon of Salamis, was one of the contenders for the arms of Achilles. These arms were to go to the most courageous Greek survivor of the battle of Troy. They went, in the event, to Odysseus. Ajax was driven mad by this slight and ran amok, dealing death to the cattle and sheep that had been seized from the Trojan farms. He then determined to kill himself. Ajax fixed his sword in the earth and threw himself on it, and the sword, repelled by what it had to do, bent itself over and so foiled its owner's attempt. At last the hero succeeded in killing himself by forcing the point of his sword into his armpit. Blood flowed on to the ground and where it rested a flower sprang up. The larkspur's claim to be this flower has, inevitably, been disputed on behalf of others, but it has won through and added the hero's name to its own (*ajacis*). According to the myth, the Greek letters 'AI AI' appear at the base of the flower's petals, AI standing for Aias Aiacides. Another version states that it stands for the simple cry of woe 'Ai, Ai!' Whatever the truth of the matter, the myth is by no means borne out by close perusal of the flower.

FORGET-ME-NOT

Romantic conceit of a thousand Victorian keep-sakes, the forget-me-not as a token of a lover's faith-fulness has its origins back in Lancastrian England. The Earl of Derby, before he became Henry IV, took up this flower, known by the French name '*souveigne vous de moy*', and let its sentiment and colours inspire a fashion – a collar of silver gilt and blue embroidered with S's. These were the initials of both 'souvenir' and the royal 'souverain' (sovereign), and the flower and the fashion were both to become popular symbols of the Lancastrian cause.

The romantic revival of the early nineteenth century brought the languishing lover back into vogue. One such is reputed to have languished more than most. He and his sweetheart were walking along the banks of the Danube on the eve of their wedding. Seeing forget-me-nots growing near the water, he climbed down to pluck the tiny blue flower for his lady love, only to be swept away to his death, calling to her desperately at the last: 'Forget me not!' The flower in question has, of course, other less sentimental names, supposedly descriptive. The botanical one, *Myosotis*, means 'mouse's ear'. 'Scorpion grass' was a popular name for many years. But the English country version of the original fourteenth-century French is with us still.

ANEMONE

There is a sudden sweep of scarlet colour each year on the lower slopes of Mount Lebanon. It comes from the glowing *Anemone coronaria* flowers at the end of the winter rains. A Syrian myth maintains that it is the blood of the demi-god Tammuz. Adonis is his Greek equivalent – the beautiful youth gored to death by Ares, a god who had changed himself into a wild boar. In the Holy Land, where the flowers grew profusely, the symbolism was adapted to Christian mythology too, which claims that the blood at the foot of the Cross was transformed into an anemone.

During the medieval Crusades a bishop of Pisa arranged for soil to be brought back from the Holy Land in the empty ships. When this was spread on the Italian ground anemones burst into flower: yet another miracle metamorphosis of the blood of the holy martyrs. As one authority comments drily, it is odd that the flower was not already known to the good bishop, for it grew in that very area.

The less flamboyant English *Anemone nemerosa*, palely nodding in the breeze, is more aptly called 'windflower' than its Greek original. 'Windflower' is a direct translation, but other local English names are charming corruptions of the Greek itself – including 'nemony', 'emony' and even 'enemy'.

LILY

The white lily – *Lilium candidum* – has been intimately associated with the Virgin Mary since the earliest days of Christianity. The flower's exterior consists of innocent white petals, 'yet within shineth the likenesse of gold'. It is the symbol of her purity and her goodness; in this role it graces the medieval pictures of the Annunciation. It decks the churches during Easter, too, declaring the joy of the Resurrection.

The lily was so admired that many another less beautiful flower gained by association with its name. 'Lilybind', 'marsh lilies', 'Lentlily' – none of these are real lilies but country names for more ordinary flowers. There was conscious flattery in the imitation. And it is only since a century or so ago that the extra name of 'Madonna' has been tacked on to the lily's name. It happened when the collector botanists began to find more new lily treasures in China and Japan.

One of these plant-hunters, Ernest Wilson, foraging near the Tibetan border in 1910, found the beautiful *Lilium regale* flowering on rocky riverside terrain. Together with his local bearers he was gathering the bulbs when a sudden rockfall crushed his leg. His attendants stretched him out on the hazardous, narrow pathway. A train of mules arrived and, as there was no diversion they could take, every single mule stepped over the valiant Wilson as he clutched his precious bulbs. He was eventually restored to the western world with a limp and the lilies. They have made his reputation.

LILY-OF-THE-VALLEY

A native flower, growing wild in Britain centuries ago, the lily-of-the-valley has a host of charming local names. One is 'Our Lady's tears', a name that originates from the belief that the tiny fragrant flowers sprang from the tears of the Virgin Mary as they fell at the foot of the cross. Then there are the seasonal names: 'May lilies', May blossoms and even 'Pache flowers'. This last, with its Easter allusion, is a little puzzling, for the white 'dangle bells' usually flower in mid-May and Whitsun is the traditional time for picking. 'Mugget' is one blunt English adaptation of the French *muguet des bois* and there are charming anglicizations of the botanical name of *Lilium convallium* given to it by sixteenth-century German apothecaries. 'Liriconfancy' and 'conval lily' are heard no more but the lily-of-the-valley has happily survived.

One English folk tale concerning this flower comes from a pocket of Sussex known as St Leonard's Forest. Dragons were said to ravage this part of the country and the saint acquired a great reputation for fighting them. His victory over one of these ferocious beasts is particularly remembered. From the blood that flowed from the dragon sprang the fragrant, delicate flower – to be known in this locality as St Leonard's lily. Even this story is not completely home-grown. The cult of St Leonard himself is supposed to have been brought to England by the Norman invaders. But whatever its source, all the folklore of the lily-of-the-valley is sweetness and light.

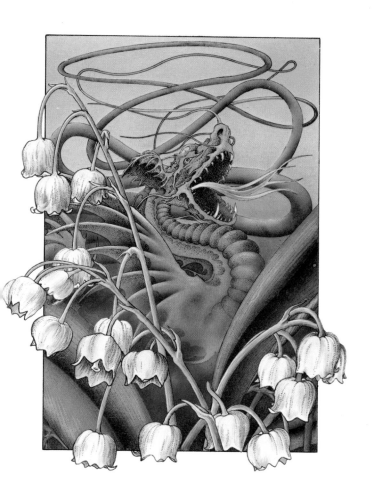

ACANTHUS

Acanthus is the architectural plant *par excellence*. It is much admired by modern landscape architects for its dramatic form, so well suited to their planting schemes. And its distinctive shape has been commemorated for all time in the classic Greek design of the Corinthian capital. The story of how it was raised to such eminence exists in several versions. In one, the architect Callimachos is supposed to have come across a specimen of the plant that had grown up through a basket. This had accidentally been covered with a tile so that the acanthus had grown up in an unusual shape. He was so impressed by the effect that he incorporated it into the design of a temple that he was building. In another, more personal, version of the story, the same architect's daughter had died, and he had put a basket of flowers on her grave. When he next came back the acanthus had grown through the basket, and thereafter served to inspire him in his art.

CHRYSANTHEMUM

The great imperial gardens of China were being tended with skill and dedication centuries before the birth of Christ, and the chrysanthemum was certainly cultivated there from at least 500 BC, when only the yellow varieties existed. But breeding techniques became more sophisticated and by the time of the Sung dynasty in the eleventh century most of the fundamental breakthroughs had been made. Seven hundred years before, the chrysanthemum had been introduced to Japan and a parallel development had taken place there.

When the nineteenth-century plant-hunters from Europe eventually managed to infiltrate themselves into these two eastern empires – where they were far from welcome – most of the work they would normally have expected to do themselves had already been done. Elsewhere in the world, they were accustomed to find simple specimens ripe for development, but the flowers of the Orient were a special case. What *was* needed, however, was a special kind of plant collector. Exceptional influence or long association with those concerned was needed for this delicate and politically dangerous task. One such man, early in the century, was John Reeves, the Chief Inspector of Tea in Canton for the East India Company and also a successful chrysanthemum shipper. The Bavarian Philipp von Siebold was an eye specialist – a great advantage, for he was welcomed for this skill in Japan, where his botanical quests were consequently tolerated. But even he overstepped the mark and was banished for a period.

Though China was its homeland, Japan had made the chrysanthemum very much its own. The flower became the imperial symbol. The flag of the Rising Sun shows, in fact, a stylized chrysanthemum emblem. Even today the Japanese emperor holds this flower in high esteem.

CLEMATIS

The native wild English *Clematis vitalba* twines itself in English hedgerows under the name of 'traveller's joy'. When the fluffy seeds of the autumn plant begin to blow, the flower's other widely known name of 'old man's beard' seems more to the point. However, this name is probably rather more than a picturesque description. The old man in question could easily be the Devil. His work, in this case, was to encourage the plant's pernicious habit of entangling and strangling anything that gets in its way.

Other local names have another story to tell. The stems of the clematis were put to good use by the provident country poor. Lengths were cut and lit up as 'smokes'. 'Boy's bacca', 'gipsy's bacca' and 'poor man's friend' – south country names for the plant – recall this popular usage.

There is pansies, that's for thoughts', Ophelia laments, reminding us of the French '*pensées*'. The wild English pansy, the *Viola tricolor*, was called by many names. One was 'herb trinity', for its three colours – a name considered blasphemous in some puritan circles. 'Heart-sease' was the prettiest and commonest of them all. It is still used to distinguish the modest wild flower from the highly developed pansy of the last two centuries. But one name, above all the others, has a very special Elizabethan appeal and is the one Shakespeare makes so memorable in *A Midsummer Night's Dream*: this is 'love-in-idleness'. All the English wild flowers of the sixteenth century seem to bloom in the 'wood near Athens' where Oberon and Titania hold sway. Here Puck is despatched by Oberon to bring back the flower:

> Yet marked I where the bolt of Cupid fell:
> It fell upon a little western flower,
> Before milk-white, now purple with love's wound,
> And maidens call it love-in-idleness,
> Fetch me that flower; the herb I showed thee once;
> The juice of it on sleeping eyelids laid
> Will make a man or woman madly dote
> Upon the next live creature that he sees.

Oberon squeezes the juice on Titania's eyelids. Titania falls madly in love with Bottom the weaver (the yokel who has himself been bewitched and now sports an ass's head). The same potion is used on two of the mortals who are in the wood that day, and the resulting complications are many. Indeed the whole plot depends on the wild pansy.

The bigger, rounder, dramatically-coloured pansy of today was originally bred by the famous Thompson, gardener to Lord Gambier, in the early nineteenth century; but though this flower may be more impressive, no romantic story attaching to it can compete with Shakespeare's magical comedy.

GERANIUM

However much the purists disapprove, people will not stop calling both pelargoniums and geraniums by the name of geranium. It was Francis Masson, disciple of the great explorer and plant-hunter Joseph Banks who sent back fifty pelargonium varieties from South Africa at the end of the eighteenth century and paved the way for the plant's great popularity with the Victorians. The archetypal plant of large-scale Victorian bedding schemes, this type is often sneered at now as being garish and, most insulting of all, 'municipal'. None the less, they can be found even in the gardens of the most sensitive souls if one looks hard enough, perhaps in a mellowed urn or artfully arranged in a mixed pot.

One type of geranium has come right back into favour recently. This is the scented-leaved geranium, the flowers of which are far less showy that the mainstream varieties. The joy of this plant is in its leaves: a gentle rub between finger and thumb releases a heady perfume. Some are rose-scented, some lemon, mint, even pine.

The legend of the origin of the *Pelargonium zonale* concerns the prophet Mahommed, who is said to have washed his garment and spread it out on a common mallow plant to dry. When the shirt was removed the plant had been miraculously changed into a bright and beautiful 'geranium'.

WALLFLOWER

In its wild state the wallflower has a happy knack of clinging to pockets of soil on the walls of old castles. But it is a flower that was domesticated and cultivated early, certainly by the sixteenth century, and was particularly popular for its pleasing scent. This scent attracts bees as well as people and the flower was happily grown by the 'husbandmen' who specialized in bee-keeping. One of its country names, 'bee-flower', confirms this reputation.

The plant was most commonly grown in traditional cottage gardens, close to the house wall just underneath the windows – a harking back, perhaps, to its wild habitat on baronial stonework.

The best-known story about the wallflower has its setting in just such a romantic place, outside a gaunt Scottish castle in the fourteenth century. Elizabeth, daughter of the Earl of March, was promised to a suitable princely suitor but preferred another, less acceptable, whose name was Scott of Tushielaw. She was kept away from him, but he managed to serenade her, disguised as a minstrel, at the foot of the castle wall. An assignation was made for her escape and she threw down a sprig of wallflower to him to indicate that she understood his message. However, when the time came for her to clamber down the rope, she slipped and fell to her death. Robert Herrick told the story, three centuries later, in verse:

> Up she got upon a wall,
> Tempting down to slide withal;
> But the silken twist untied,
> So she fell, and, bruised, she died.

In Herrick's version, the lady then turns instantly into a wallflower, while the earlier tale is less fanciful: according to this, the mourning lover wandered through Europe as a minstrel, wearing the wallflower in his cap in memory of his loss.

PRIMROSE

Sweet spring flower of the grassy banks, the little primrose had a special kind of fame thrust upon it at the end of the last century. Benjamin Disraeli, the Conservative statesman, had claimed many years before his ennoblement as Lord Beaconsfield that the primrose was his favourite flower. Queen Victoria knew of his preference and sent him a spring bunch regularly.

This custom was kept fairly low-key until the day of Disraeli's death, on 19 April 1881, when a primrose wreath was placed on his coffin. The flowers had been picked near the royal palace of Osborne on the Isle of Wight and the card attached was in the Queen's own hand: 'His favourite flowers; from Osborne; a tribute of affectionate regard from Queen Victoria.'

A statue of the former Prime Minister was shortly commissioned and unveiled. Conservative members of Parliament, to a man, sported a primrose buttonhole for the occasion. It was then a short step to the formation of the Primrose League, a Conservative ginger group of considerable influence in its day. Their badges and jewellery featured the primrose in the designs. Every year the League celebrated Primrose Day on the anniversary of Disraeli's death, when the flower was worn. Thus it was that the primrose enjoyed extraordinary political significance for a considerable number of years.

FUCHSIA

Everything about the fuchsia – its distinctive colour, its very special showy style – is redolent of the High Victorian society that took it to its heart. Yet the fuchsia was discovered in the wild habitats of Central and South America at the tail end of the eighteenth century.

The story of how it was first developed commercially has many charming elements – mother love, chance and entrepreneural success, for example – but is dubious in the extreme. James Lee, a famous nurseryman of Hammersmith, chanced to pass by a humble dockland cottage in Wapping, on the outskirts of London. There on the windowsill stood an exotic fuchsia. The plantsman discovered that the owner was the mother of a sailor who had brought the plant back for her from San Domingo. Lee bargained hard to buy it but the lady was reluctant. She eventually settled for eighty guineas and the promise of a rooted cutting. Lee proceeded to raise 300 cuttings, which he sold for one guinea each.

A more sober version has it that a Captain Firth brought two plants back from South America and presented them to the Royal Botanic Gardens at Kew.

Throughout the nineteenth-century the Victorian plantsmen carried out a host of breeding and hybridization experiments with the fuchsia, while elsewhere, on Great Britain's Celtic fringes, something quite different was happening: the fuschia was becoming naturalized. The Atlantic coastline still glows with the unique deep pink of the fuchsia in bloom.

DAHLIA

In the Aztec gardens of Mexico the cocoxochitl flourished brightly for centuries before, in 1789, specimens were sent from the Botanic Gardens of Mexico City to Spain. There Abbé Cavanilles, who ran the gardens of the Escorial in Madrid, renamed it in European fashion after Dr Anders Dahl, a Swedish botanist. Specimens were sent on to France's Jardin des Plantes, and in both Madrid and Paris, it was hoped that the dahlia tubers could be raised as vegetables – possible tasty alternatives to the potato.

Such hopes were eventually dashed, for the flavour was not agreeable, but the bright dahlia flowers were much admired and coveted. In early experiments, there were problems in cultivating the plant. Many rotted and died from unsuitable treatment simply because the dahlia's needs were not understood at that time. Those who eventually succeeded in raising them were loath to share the secret of their triumphs with others. Empress Joséphine, who took great delight in her gardens at Malmaison, tended her dahlias with personal dedication. One story tells how a lady-in-waiting, refused a single tuber by Joséphine, encouraged her lover to bribe a gardener to steal a hundred of them. When the plot was discovered, the lady-in-waiting was dismissed, the lover banished from Court and the gardener fired. It is said that Joséphine in her anger then dug in her dahlia beds and would have nothing more to do with them. For some years the plant remained rare, difficult to cultivate, and expensive. But by the first decade of the nineteenth century, the turning point had come. Seeds from a different source in Mexico were successfully raised in Germany and the Low Countries, whereupon the dahlia was set fair for prolific breeding and in due course widespread popularity.

FOXGLOVE

The foxglove is a powerful plant – even for foxes. If one is cunning enough to wear the petals on his paws he will have trapped the flower's magic and will be able to creep silently up to the chicken house. No one will be able to catch him at it. The fairies have a very special claim on foxglove magic. It was really their plant – they just let the foxes use it. Local names such as 'fairy fingers' and 'witch's thimble', 'dead women's thimbles', 'Puck fingers' and many more are indicative of its magic associations. The plant was supposedly used by fairies and could be turned against them by intrepid mortals. The juice of the plant had power to bring back a child that had been taken away by the fairies. And if an unwelcome changeling had been left with people by the fairies it could be got rid of by rubbing foxglove juice on the fairy child.

SNOWDROP

The snowdrop, white and welcome before the coming of the spring, is fêted as the Fair Maid of February and intimately associated in the Christian calendar with Candlemas. A symbol of purity, the flower was brought into Lady chapels and churches on 2 February, the day of that feast, to celebrate the Purification of the Virgin. This explains the flower's old English name of 'Candlemas bells' and also supports the view that the flower is not a wild native of England but was originally nurtured in monastery gardens for this ritual use.

The folklore of the snowdrop includes another, more fanciful tale. Adam and Eve faced a bleak, snowy, northern winter as, banished from the Garden of Eden, they trudged away. Eve fell behind, exhausted and discouraged, believing that life would henceforth be all winter. When she could go no further an angel appeared and succeeded in convincing her that the weather would eventually change, that there was such a thing as spring. The angel proved the point dramatically by transforming some falling snowflakes into white flowers of spring. Reassured by the sight of the snowdrops, Eve took heart and found the courage to travel onwards. This story shows why, in the language of flowers, the snowdrop means hope.

DAISY

The daisy is a simple, artless flower, token of an idyllic country childhood. Somerset calls it baby's pet, Yorkshire 'bairnwort'. Even today children have a special affection for daisies. The gardener may regard them as expendable, ridding his lawns of them by means of herbicide and mower, but at least their prolific growth means they can be picked with impunity to make daisy chains: a thumbnail through the stems and they can be quickly threaded together. Such activities are the very essence of happy childhood: 'Buttercups and daisies, Oh the pretty flowers; Coming ere the Springtime, To tell of happy hours.' Another meadow game is to chant, 'He loves me, he loves me not', counting while each petal is pulled off in turn until the final petal decides which is true.

The childhood theme persists. A fairy by the name of Milkah fed her royal foster-child with daisy roots to keep him a miniature man. And the juice is reputed to keep a dog puppy-sized, too.

Like a good child, the daisy opens and shuts its eyes promptly with the sun, which enchanted the poet Chaucer. The daisy's current name is very close to the beautiful medieval original of 'dayseye' that the poet celebrated.

> That wel by reason men hit calle may
> The 'dayseye' or elles the 'ye of day',
> The emperice and flour of floures all.

Gone yet not forgotten,
although we are apart,
your spirit lives within me,
forever in My Heart

Bold And
Home Ma

COLUMBINE

The two legitimate names for this cottage garden flower are aquilegia, after the eagle (*aquila*), and columbine, after the dove. These are both explained by the pretty – and unusual – shape of the petals and spurs of the flower, that are now, in the modern hybrid varieties, even more noticeable. Other names, from various parts of rural England, include 'stocking and shoe', 'Granny's bonnet' and 'fool's cap' – and it takes no more than an imaginative glance at the flower to explain them. But one name, *herba leonis*, is less obvious. It was said that if you rubbed your hands on the flower you would be given lion-like courage (lions were supposed to feed on columbines). There is a simple mythological connection for this puzzling attribute in the form of Aphrodite, goddess of love, whom the ancient Greeks associated with both lions and doves.

VIOLET

Cultivated in ancient Persian gardens to make the drink sherbet, eaten in Rome with lemon and orange, used in sedatives and potions, the utility of the violet has never been allowed to overshadow its winning looks. Symbol of the great city of Athens, it was cultivated there so successfully that it was on sale in the streets in every season of the year, to be made into wreaths and chaplets.

However, it was Napoleon Bonaparte who created the most remarkable violet cult, one that lasted far longer that the legendary 100 days of his exile on Elba that began the whole affair. As he left for the island he promised his supporters that he would return 'with the violets in the spring'. Overnight the violet became the Bonapartists' symbol, and indeed the password that identified those who longed for his return. Bunches were worn in his honour, violet accessories were created and mementoes depicted Bonaparte with the violet device. The toast was to 'Corporal Violet who will return in the spring'.

And this he did. Women greeted him with violets when he reached the south of France, and again on his arrival in Paris in March 1815. Even after this event, the cult lived on. Out of fashion under the Bourbon restoration, violets were back in favour during the Second Empire, enthusiastically taken up by Empress Eugénie. And at the last the Napoleonic violet poignantly appeared in the incongruous setting of Chislehurst in Kent for the funeral service in 1879 of the Prince Imperial, son of the dispossessed Napoleon III and the Empress Eugénie.

ACKNOWLEDGEMENTS

Of the many books which have provided source material for *Heritage of Flowers* the author is especially indebted to the following:

Flowers and their Histories, Alice M. Coats (Hulton Press)
Flowers in History, Peter Coats (Weidenfeld & Nicolson)
Variations on a Garden, Robin Lane Fox (Macmillan)
Poorman's Nosegay, Lesley Gordon (Collins/Harvill)
The Development of Garden Flowers, Richard Gorer (Eyre & Spottiswoode)
An Englishmen's Flora, Geoffrey Grigson (Hart Davis)
The Plant Hunters, Tyler Whittle (Heinemann).

Hutchinson & Co. (Publishers) Ltd
An imprint of the Hutchinson Publishing Group
3 Fitzroy Square, London W1P 6JD
Hutchinson Group (Australia) Pty Ltd
30–32 Cremorne Street, Richmond South, Victoria 3121
PO Box 151, Broadway, New South Wales 2007
Hutchinson Group (NZ) Ltd
32–34 View Road, PO Box 40-086, Glenfield, Auckland 10
Hutchinson Group (SA) Pty Ltd
PO Box 337, Bergvlei 2012, South Africa
First published 1980
Designed and produced for Hutchinson & Co. by

BELLEW&HIGTON

Bellew & Higton Publishers Ltd
19–21 Conway Street London W1P 6JD
Copyright © Bellew & Higton Publishers Ltd 1980
ISBN 0 09 143180 8
Printed and bound in Spain

by Printer Industria Gráfica S.A.
Provenza, 388/Barcelona, San Vicente dels Horts 1980
Depósito Legal B. 16013 – 1980